W9-BXL-570

MATH ACADEMY

ADDITION
ON THE
MENU

By Kirsty Holmes

CRABTREE
PUBLISHING COMPANY
WWW.CRABTREEBOOKS.COM

CRABTREE
PUBLISHING COMPANY
WWW.CRABTREEBOOKS.COM

Author:
Kirsty Holmes
Editorial director:
Kathy Middleton
Editors:
William Anthony, Janine Deschenes
Proofreader:
Crystal Sikkens
Graphic design:
Ian McMullen
Prepress technician:
Katherine Berti
Print coordinator:
Katherine Berti

All images are courtesy of Shutterstock.com, unless otherwise specified. With thanks to Getty Images, Thinkstock Photo, and iStockphoto.

Front Cover: Ahmad Ihsan, Andrey_Kuzmin, wk1003mike, glenda, no_frames

Interior: Background – ngaga. Characters: Maya: Rajesh Narayanan. Zoe: Dave Pot. Robert: Shift Drive. Abdul: Ahmad Ihsan. Professor Tengent: Roman Samborskyi. Cy-Bud: AlesiaKan. 5 – eurobanks. Iasha. 6 – Hayati Kayhan, artnLera, MF production. 7 – Bakhtiar Zein. 8 – Creatus. 10 – Mega Pixel, Stilesta.11 – Gelpi, Tom Wang, siro46. Lewis – Cookie Studio. Dee Dee – LightField Studios. Kush: Gratsias Adhi Hermawan. Ling: GOLFX. Paige: Oleksandr Zamuruiev. Katie: LightField Studios. 12 – STILLFX. 13 – Cheers Group, Kyselova Inna. 14 – rvlsoft, Sergey Peterman. 15 – bogdandimages. 16 – Studioimagen73, paulista. 21 – AtlasStudio. 22 – reud, artnLera. 23 – baibaz, SOMMAI, akepong srichaichana, Tiger Images

All facts, statistics, web addresses, and URLs in this book were verified as valid and accurate at time of writing. No responsibility for any changes to external websites or references can be accepted by either the author or publisher.

Library and Archives Canada Cataloguing in Publication

Title: Addition on the menu / by Kirsty Holmes.
Names: Holmes, Kirsty, author.
Description: Series statement: Math academy | Includes index.
Identifiers: Canadiana (print) 20200394037 |
  Canadiana (ebook) 2020039407X |
  ISBN 9781427130099 (hardcover) |
  ISBN 9781427130136 (softcover) |
  ISBN 9781427130174 (HTML)
Subjects: LCSH: Addition—Juvenile literature.
Classification: LCC QA115 .H65 2021 | DDC j513.2/11—dc23

Library of Congress Cataloging-in-Publication Data

Available at the Library of Congress

Crabtree Publishing Company

www.crabtreebooks.com   1–800–387–7650
Published by Crabtree Publishing Company in 2021
© 2020 BookLife Publishing Ltd.

Printed in the U.S.A./022021/CG20201123

Published in Canada
Crabtree Publishing
616 Welland Ave.
St. Catharines, Ontario
L2M 5V6

Published in the United States
Crabtree Publishing
347 Fifth Ave
Suite 1402-145
New York, NY 10016

CONTENTS

Words that are bold, like **this**, can be found in the glossary on page 24.

ATTENDANCE

Another day at Math Academy has begun. Time to take attendance! Meet some students in class 301.

Maya
Favorite subject:
Place value

Zoë
Favorite subject:
Counting in groups

Professor Tangent

Ali
Favorite subject:
Addition

Robert
Favorite subject:
Subtraction

Today's lesson is all about **addition**. The students will learn answers to these questions.

- What is addition?

- Can we add more than two numbers together?

- How can a number line help us add?

Math Academy is a school especially for kids who love math and solving problems.

Do I hear the bell?

MORNING LESSON

Each morning, the students in class 301 send tomorrow's lunch order to the cafeteria. Today, it is Robert's turn to bring the list to Chef Addie.

LUNCH ORDER
Class: 301

Burgers	9
Sandwiches	8
Fries	17
Salads	7
Oranges	11
Apples	13

Professor Tangent, I can't find the list with tomorrow's lunch order!

Professor Tangent is extremely smart. He can do all kinds of difficult math. He never needs to use his fingers to **count**! Unfortunately, he is also very forgetful.

I have no idea where I put the list! Maybe it is in this box under my paper shredder.

LUNCHTIME

Oh no! Professor Tangent has accidentally put class 301's lunch order in the paper shredder! The piece of paper has been cut into little strips. It takes the students all morning to gather all of the strips.

We will have to try to put the piece of paper back together!

Robert lines up the strips in the shape of a piece of paper. But how will the students know if they have found all of the pieces? What if someone's lunch order is missing? Cy-Bud has an idea.

We can add up the lunch orders! If the **total** number of orders match the total number of students, then no strips of paper are missing.

Adding is putting two or more numbers together to make a new number. Professor Tangent shows the students an example.

> Imagine you have two strawberries in one hand and two strawberries in the other hand. Adding them together **equals** four strawberries.

$$2 + 2 = 4$$

There are 24 students in class 301. If the classmates can find 24 lunch orders in the strips of paper, no orders are missing. Time to get adding!

=24

MAKE IT RIGHT WITH MATH

Each student gets a choice of fruit with their lunch. They can choose an orange or an apple. Robert can see the fruit orders on different strips of paper.

Oranges 🍊 11

Apples 🍎 13

> First, let's add up the number of fruit orders. Then, we can add up the number of main meal and side orders.

Adding the number of oranges and the number of apples should equal 24. Let's see!

Oranges 🍊 [11]

+

Apples 🍎 [13]

Oranges and Apples [24]

$$11+13=24$$

+
The plus sign is the **symbol** for addition

=
The equals sign is the symbol that shows the total

There are no missing fruit orders!

ALI ADDS IT UP

Next, the students need to add up the main meals. The strips say there are nine orders for burgers and eight orders for sandwiches. Let's see if they add up to 24.

Burgers 9

Sandwiches 8

Burgers and Sandwiches 17

We only have 17 main meals. There are some orders missing!

$9+8=17$

Look! Maya found a note. It says that seven **vegetarian** meals need to be added to the list. The students add these meals to the total of burgers and sandwiches.

To Chef Addie,
Please add 7 vegetarian main meals for class 301.

Thanks,
Professor Tangent

$$17 + 7 = 24$$

Now we have the right number of main meals!

Finally, the students need to add up the side orders.
There are seven orders for salads, and 17 orders for fries.

Salads 🥗 7

Fries 🍟 17

Addition is not always easy for me. Can you show me a different way to add?

Ali wants to help Robert. He explains that a number line can make it easier to add numbers. This number line goes up to 30. First, the students find one number they need to add. There are 17 orders for fries. Ali points to the number 17 on the number line.

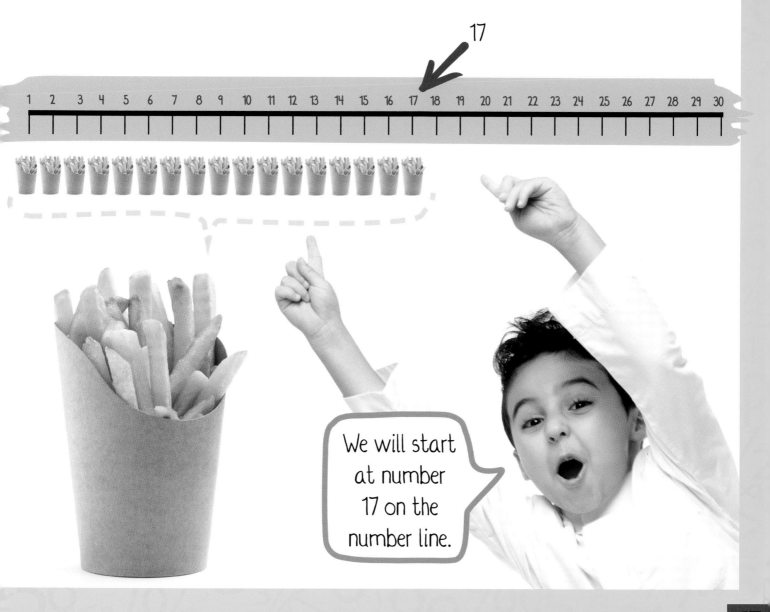

17

1 2 3 4 5 6 7 8 9 10 11 12 13 14 15 16 17 18 19 20 21 22 23 24 25 26 27 28 29 30

We will start at number 17 on the number line.

To add the number of salad orders, the students will start counting from 17. There are seven orders for salads. Starting at 17, Ali moves his finger seven places along the number line.

Total =24

1 2 3 4 5 6 7 8 9 10 11 12 13 14 15 16 17 18 19 20 21 22 23 24 25 26 27 28 29 30

7

The total is 24!

17+7=24

To add a third number, you can keep counting along the number line.

Wow! The number line makes adding easier for me. Now I can see that the total is 24. No side orders are missing!

11 oranges + 13 apples = 24

9 burgers + 8 sandwiches + 7 vegetarian meals = 24

17 fries + 7 salads = 24

Now that they have all the correct orders, Professor Tangent writes out the list again. Ali takes it to Chef Addie. She is glad to see the new list, but there is one problem.

The list is too late! Luckily, Chef Addie had a back-up plan. Tomorrow, class 301 will have pizza for lunch!

HOMEWORK

Can you add up Chef Addie's pizza toppings?

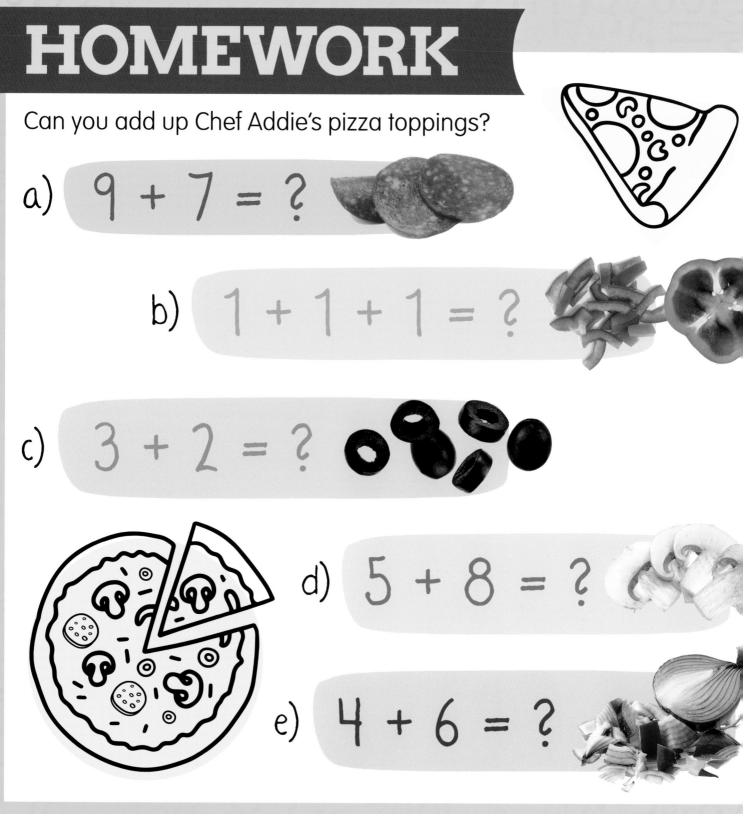

a) $9 + 7 = ?$

b) $1 + 1 + 1 = ?$

c) $3 + 2 = ?$

d) $5 + 8 = ?$

e) $4 + 6 = ?$

Use the number line to add up the number of desserts below.

| 1 | 2 | 3 | 4 | 5 | 6 | 7 | 8 | 9 | 10 | 11 | 12 | 13 | 14 | 15 | 16 | 17 | 18 | 19 | 20 | 21 | 22 | 23 | 24 | 25 | 26 | 27 | 28 | 29 | 30 |

$$9 + 7 + 8 + 5 = ?$$

GLOSSARY

ADDITION Adding two or more numbers together to make a new number

COUNT Add objects in order to find a total

EQUALS In math, a word or symbol that means the total of numbers on one side is equal to the total of numbers on the other side

NUMBER LINE A straight line with numbers evenly spaced along it

SYMBOL A shape or mark that represents, or stands for, something else

TOTAL The whole amount or number of something

VEGETARIAN Without meat

INDEX